Conte

CW00890829

Maureen Sangster was born in Aberdeen in 1954. She has lived in Scotland all her life except for three years spent teaching English in Nigeria.

Until recently, she worked as a part-time tutor with The Workers' Educational Association in Fife. She now lives in Edinburgh with her cat.

Acknowledgements

Some of these poems have previously appeared in: *Chapman, Fresh Oceans* (Stramullion), *Original Prints IV* (Polygon), *Virago New Poets 1993, Different People* (Straightline Publications), *Pomegranate Anthology* (1992), *A Mindin'* (Michael Bruce Poetry Competition Anthology 1993), *West Coast Magazine, Understanding, 4D, Graffiti, Northlight, Northwords* and *Lines Review.*

The author would like to thank the following people and organisations: the Scottish Arts Council for a bursary in 1993 which gave her time to put this collection together; Kenneth Storrie for his support; members of The Fife Writers' Group, Splinters Women's Writing Group, Pomegranate Women's Writing Group and The School of Poets.

Good Behaviour

Food is Sex:
and feeling sick
in the stomach
is disgust at sex

Food slips over
straightforwardly
requires no backward
looks or apologies

Food is the nipple
cracked and sore
my mother's nipple
I couldn't have

Food is mine
Above all other
certainties, cramming
my mouth is definite

Food like sex
disgusts me: its
bulk bulges in me
I fear memory

Food seals lips
and opens lips:
it becomes waste
its retention is ugly

Whom do I eat
when I eat, whose
fleshy point of return
do I savour? Suck?

Food divides me:
the me that wants
to love and make love
with you from the me

1

that wants only
an empty room
the hidden snacks
to attack

Before bed – separate
beds as long as
Food is bad to me
and I try to be

Good.

Sea Dream

Sea stone sea dream
sea gun stun she walks
her smug head (supremo poll tax head)
coiffured, her Marie Antoinette demeanour
Sea wall sea sand sea shore
now she stands delivering oratory
to a clutch of gypsies
herded by police outside their caravans
'Seize litter,' she is saying 'We must get back to…'
Sea tides sea fish sea shells
against her intoning 'Nothing wrong
with the creation of wealth…'
her 'Re-establishment of family values' sea past sea
history sea fury
Crack the power part its features
her tongue extend it till all
the vile undigested pain flows out
her sad disowned subjugated mother
her imperial father a twisted
life
oh let it go – that sadness
           that madness
that exclusion of –
           sea
           sea
           cleanse Margaret!

First Steps –

after the miscarriage

I am left with
nothing
but nothing
a cave where
nothing rests,
the walls dank.

If I am frightened of
not crying at anything,
it is because
nothing is here.

The monster clock's face
I don't want to look at

yet the afternoon is
half-ended,
its shivering,

but nothing is connected to
the emptiness –
not a child frilled
going by on wheels –

how people's odd
hands hover.
Are they going to
hold, help
no one along the bus?

The Gap

They take out what is dead inside.
This happens.
The white coat says, 'I'm sorry.'
It is not a day of decisions then.
They operate.

The day before I had wondered
at the wind and rain swayed trees
trees out of the centre of town
trees not in the country
long worn-out arms going
backwards and forwards not pin-
pointing, on a darkening night, wettening.

A hole to go into, not understanding
profound as on one night a heartbeat
the next night, none.
At first, two small humans,
a clutch of hearts on the hospital drive
and inside one, a derangement of the senses,
pushed pulled unchoosing
her blood as yet unexposed
not sloshed over the gap

bed bed bed beds
clean sheeted happenings
an awful eyeful of women
Slowly up the ward comes
the distended stomach of a lack of womb.
She smiles
and then I cramped and
found hills and dips of pain and relief
and lost the good safe clock.
What? What is coming out?

Next day, the white coat
from its scan, its map
said there was certainty.
This was not a day for decisions then
as all the days before had been –
abortion or a mummy?
What dies when someone else is born?
This was a day for an operation.
They evacuate the womb

but afterwards at home
the monstrous cow rushed out of the womb,
wrong, bellowing her terror!
A dream. I got up. Then I met
in the bathroom, staring at me,
an animal, an abortion,
the silken survival of a cat that
howled and fled as I screamed.

Travel

But the maps were huge,
the room went.

The red line of our journey
cut through countries.
A swirl of contours,
a gasp of waters
tugged us in.

A town on a boundary!
Heat of double being
strong division.

Afraid to go?
but oh, those maps
tumbling seas of paper
flung us forward
We'd go, we'd go
up high tracks spiked
with signs

the maps were huge
but in our pockets we placed
their seas and hills
and our forgotten room.

Woman

Men in the village are mutterin
mutterin, muttrin 'bout
the woman in the village.
Men in the village are judgin
judgin, judgin
the woman in the village –
she open
open to the touch
open to the touch of strangers.
Jealous bark of their anger
stokin
stokin to a crazy blazin
spit in the beer
beat with the fist
mad in the eye
bad bondin.
They'd rape her,
rape her, rape her
in their mind's dark clearin
for a woman like that
a woman like that
ain't got a wound for bleedin
ain't got a wound for bleedin.

I know her, I know her
I know this woman, she my sister.
Yes, she open
open to the touch
but open to the touch of livin.
Beautiful? yes
but her beauty
she know how to leave it.
Kindly? yes
and her kindness
she feed it,
this woman, my sister
my sister, my sister

an' at the dance,
at the fes-ti-val
she give to the spirit
not to the priest,
she dance with the dance
not with the chief
this woman, my sister,
my sister, my sister
is packin it in, she
learnin! leavin
the paths in the village,
going in her own direction
open to the touch of fun
open to the touch of sun
open to a world to come.

The men in the village
can't make her.
The men in the village can't take her
so they take her, rape her
in the dark outside the village.
Hard lesson in bleedin
hard lesson in bleedin.

Oh I'm sore 'bout my sister.
I'm sore 'bout my sister
her breakin, her bleedin
which men in the dark ain't seein.
I'm cryin for my sister,
I'm cryin for a world that's twisted,
I'm cryin by the grave of the future
if it's only hate that's breedin.
Is it only hate that's breedin?

Through the Looking Glass

through the looking
glass: your breasts
aren't flat,
their nipples startle.
after a drunken night
out we find ourselves
in bed together. When
will your boyfriend intrude?
When will mine? of course
we have
gone
through the looking glass
down
the
rabbit
hole into the Time Machine
forwards backwards
women
dream of this
it always is yet
Tomorrow
we'll begin again
our false liaison
with The World. Muddled by
the brrrrr
the whirr
our hoarse voices
will grasp the safe re-
lief of sameness
and in the office break
neither you nor I
shall mention us
but, desperately, through
our coats
our scarves
our rings
our skirts
our shoes
our hair

our colours
our breasts
we'll advertise
a man has you, a man has me
oh, my love, our lie!

Mr Bishop on the Back-Shift

I see the grass
the bold nasturtiums
orange yellow only
a few dark red ones
I see the apple tree
the long top branches
swaying in the wind

I dig my spade
into earth round the tree
clunk clunk goes the spade
cutting through the earth

I have no plan in mind
the sun beats down
the greenhouse
reflects sheets
on the clothes whirligig
reflects our house the nasturtiums
the swaying apple tree branches

what a muddle
these reflections are
I can't dig them over
pull any of them out
like weeds. I should

grow tomato plants
blank out the confusion
the glass brings

Inside/Outside

Let the hexagonal glass jar display its water
                                     for as long as it wants
showing the liquid level shimmering inside.
They won't let me inside
their houses gardens shrink in size
the tiles bush thatch
the eaves drop
the cosiness is to keep me out.
Oh I am cunt
with things inside
deep iris eyes unmentioned
if I could be sick, retch my cunt like a stomach
the fish the rigid frog
the wet dry story would be told.

The spikey vegetation darts its growths inside the glass dome
showing blurred green through glass dazzled by the sun.
I can't get in through the man
tight like the flattest of all worlds
thin like the flattest piece of wood.
It is untold what is inside him –
sometimes all is wrong and I want a severance of skin,
to lie him on his stomach
and part the cheeks of his behind as any legs are opened –
what colours of impossibility are always tantalisingly here!
If this is aggression or rather what cannot be
still it is welcome –
if I could enter with a penile say what visions would arise?

Ducks Talk on Blackford Pond

Ducks talk on Blackford pond
now the intruders have gone.
Theirs, a dark pool – criss-crossed
by black twigs on trees through which I look
down at the deserted path round the pond.
Ducks talk on Blackford pond
when the intruders have gone.

I talk and find my heart
inside the black treasures of the trees
and hurry up the path to
a streak of sunset in the sky.
I can talk when ducks talk
and cry on Blackford pond
when the intruders have gone.

Ducks cry on Blackford pond
when the intruders have gone.
Some rise into the sky,
vanish in the dark hill rising.
No one comes. I draw a tree, a path,
the silent swell of hillside,
the downtownward path.
The town is chimneys, darkness, lights.
Arthur's Seat blackens as I draw.
The wind is hard
at the pages of my drawing book.
What I have I draw – it's me
when my intruders have gone.

In the Bath

The bath in the London household
is yellow, big and old.
It stands in the customary silence
of traffic making inroads into the house.
It's late morning, a day off
from her job in the Imperial War Museum.
The sun and pot-pourri fill
a little dish on the window-sill.
The curled up cat unfurls herself
and starts to lick between her claws.
The bath is a wide-bottomed boat,
in which, blowing smoke-rings, Caroline begins to float
above the Thames. Settling down with clouds, she dreams of
numerous days off from the Imperial War Museum.

A Poem for Mary Oliver
Artist and Teacher

she has released our selves
birds from an aviary
the pecked at competitive mesh
in tatters, our small bodies

hurl outwards the shapes we find
amaze us unknowing things
here is the shape that haunted us
in our dim imprisonment

here is a texture we cried over
in dreams for it touched us
there is sky blue and many blues
and wind our brush dips into

the aviary was no place to be
this space where selves fly
straight to a tree is our home now
where our eyes, released, see

Mother in the North

Mother in the north, your ashes burn
making a bonfire of your grave
Visitors to the cemetery turn
to see the bonnie sparks, the turbulence you make

Mother in the north, your body's wakening
screaming like a witch who feels the heat
She shouts out loud her defiance as she's dying
Oh mother, shake off your false beliefs

Oh mother, I was busy busy sailing
on the river of the sky, that band of light
when fiery faces stopped me, saying
You are her daughter, Rage is your birthright

So mother in the north here I'm standing
I've travelled up the east coast to your grave
Long time have my hands held the cold rocks of mourning
but now I need the reddening heat of flames

Why, mother, did I never know you
you, the witch, the wood I could have danced inside?
Though I lay curled up inside your swollen belly
when I came out, I ran away to hide

Mother, your troubled grave is settling
like a Viking funeral here on earth
The wealth of flames is deeply inviting
I board the burning plot of your rebirth

The Church's arms were brutal and ready
to stick Sin into your skin and to your heart
Duty became your only daughter
and she and I were always far apart

But, mother, we are witches now together
I, above the earth, and you, beneath the ground
We'll tug at the roots of new religion
Our pagan pact is strong, our voices loud

Mother in the north, you are sacred
the wood encircled by the ripening corn
recovering the memories you gave me
of the land, the countryside where you were born

I bend down and place my flowers
on your grave. I ignore the sky.
This is a homecoming, returning
to my mother earth, the faith that never dies.

In the Fish-House

The haddock blocks
easy gutting. It requires
longer than a holiday job to learn
the slick incisions
with the gutting-knife
about the three-pronged structure
of its back-bone.

The herring is simple
letting in
one deft stroke of the knife
along its belly
and releasing
its soft pinkish underworld
so easily
a new girl at the table
piles up gutted mounds
in her first afternoon

and at her feet
pails with scaly handles
fill up with
shoals of tiny tails
and heads brimful with eyes
and loads of flat back-bones.

By the burnie that feeds the muckle DEE

I bided by a burnie
far I aften saw a bairnie
swimmin throu the watter
an fechtin wi the fish.

He blethered wi the fishermen
nicked the ham frae oot their sandwiches
weel, he grew plump an bonnie
an oh, I wanted him fur me

So I took tae standin patient
on the bank, laden wi a thermos
an ither temptin goodies,
I thocht I'd get him throu his greed

But he pit oot his tongue rudely
an passed by ma misfortune
an I've heard, syne, that he crawled oot
at the Palace up the DEE.

I've still nae got a bairnie
I keep ma vigil by the burnie
an I try nae tae bear a grudge
agin the Prince, the faither up the DEE

but if bairnies are gettin choosey
fur status an fur money
there'll be gey mony left standin
by the burnie that feeds the muckle DEE.

Being Intimate

O when ye pit yer hand doon
tae the place it fits
it feels like gid sweet sherry works
bamboozlin tae the wits

I've rin oot frae ma human coat
I'm like a plant that slips
I'm slippin frae the tabletop
Ma pot'll drop! Ma pot'll drop!

I hae three breasts upon ma chest
Yer sweet head's one o them
Ye flung ma jumper far enough
but now ye're makin friends

I hae a flight o seagulls
that's liftin through ma head
O catch their wings, those lovely things
and tuck yer hands beneath
their soft white breasts

You curve ma back
I shape yer arm
We're sure of what we do
We're rapidly escapin frae
a box o a bedroom

The angles are a altered
the ceilin's bashin through
O knobble nibble knobble
knobble knobble nibble noo!

That window looks fair gackit
Has it got a new view too?
Instead o streets an city muck
does it look to frothy blue?

For I feel we are on holiday
nae in a city pit
so unrestrained
let's begin again
being intimate

Fields Needing Angels

Fields needing angels are full of foaming fury,
The harvest, like a whirlwind, never stays,
So, knocking on the North Sea, they ask for static glory,
Fields needing angels keep yesterday, today.

Horizons shimmer but the haystacks built are harnessed.
A bird, like a pebble, drops to tap the grain
And, fields demanding glory will howl until they're witnessed,
Yet, how silently, in guilty rage, the labourers stack the bales.

And fields needing angels will lash their foaming fury
Until in later prisons they shall meet their dead
Who, turned into good monsters, daughters, not a morning
    glory
Will have buds so unlike roses there'll be no baby's head.

Oh fields needing angels, how much they need angels
But not descended from the farming God to whom they pray
They need angels of compassion who will split their staunch
    division
Between men and women, rich and poor and give ALL equal
    say

But those distant fields of fury preserve anger that no glory
Took matters into its hands, praised them for what they'd
    gained.
What? their miserable remittances wrenched from workers'
    hands and faces,
Our angels must resist land lust and land gain, RECLAIM!

To Christ

Oh Christ, ye're juist a meenister
ye're nae bloody eese tae me
ye winna come an mak
ma mither's tea

a stuck up little mannie
bawkin oot yer words o Love
for God's sake, come doon tae earth
an wear the oven glove

fit wye is this, Messiah,
that I maun lose ma life
carin for ma mither
fan ma brither's got – a wife?

if ye'd come roon on Sunday
gie me a helpin hand
one shot o handlin the commode
an you wid understand

ma life is juist a constant roon
o meals and bloody peels
if the hand o God is in this, Christ,
it's a mystery nae revealed

Aberdeen

No one can take
Aberdeen from me
that cold grey city

I only come
at Xmas-time
when bleakness
seems a grand design –

chill air –
the seagulls rising
from the harbour
crying by the River Dee

This Xmas
a swooping seagull
dropped near me
its half-finished greed
I shuddered

at the exposed backbone
the sightless eyeball's sheen

Aberdeen
a cruel inset eye
a curious me

The Tree

from the tree in the wood
to the shed by the sea

from the sky round its head
to being at sea

from the grey of its bark
to the orange glow of its planks

from birdsong to hammering
in long firm nails

from the skill of nest-makers
to the craft of boat-builders

from the upright stance in the wood
to being held in a vice

from nature to nature
from wood to the sea

from growing to sailing
to be to be to be

a half-leaf shape
a new boat launched onto the sea

Landscape

I wrench from flat landscapes
perspectives, shadows, tones.
They will be vital later,
viewed.

You turn the pages of my drawing-book,
inspect the colours used,
pronounce some tones achieved.
You like considering
pictures, where lines are placed.
My pictures you discover are
adequate.

But underneath their shapes of
munching cows and purple mountains
I have hidden dreams
of you,
of loneliness,
of a loch at night,
drawn in black and blue
like a deep bruise.

When Men Are Fully Dressed

When men are fully dressed,
they are different from when
they are only wearing socks
but
when men are fully dressed,
you can see that strip of flesh
below the trouser bottom,
above the sock top.
It is weak, tender, gentle
reminding you of the bedroom
late at night –
static –
the dark gripping the inside of the room
the moon – who knows?
and the man standing only in his socks,
tender, gentle,
bare lovely skin exposed.

In the Bush

I can see
all animals
clearly.
A leopard
is just spots
joined up
by my eye.
But you,
with a banana grin,
disappearing up into the coconut palm
put me
out of sight.

The Prostitutes of Les Halles

With bold cold stares
The prostitutes of Les Halles stand
Pulling in their jackpot, sullenly

They are statues
But like reflexive verbs
Go back, unsmiling, upon themselves

Raising two fingers to a man
To indicate the cost
Of caged indifference

The Watcher

I am grey, unlit, the watcher
as snow, enchantment, gathers up a couple
into the freedom of its soft white street

they grab snow from off their car roof
press hard and quick and fling snowballs
not meaning to hit each other at all

the still street is a flat ski-slope,
is a ballroom floor – See how the man swings
round and round, arms out like wings

I can hear their laughter as I stand
in the dark bedroom, looking out
What have I become but a sullen spy

on the build-up of snow, on the beauty of snow
on the way its cold charm entices lovers

a spy, on a landscape I can't walk into –
with its swirling effects of change and motion

Out With Eoin

Could you leave
your bag here
the attendant shouted
on Eoin

Eoin
while we
and a family of four
(all of us with bags)
climbed the art gallery's stairs
freely

Could you leave
your bag here
you young person
you black leather jacketed
young person
you person with
white paint painted onto
that black leather jacket

Could you leave
your bag here
the attendant said
and Eoin descended the stairs
to do so

and did so
and the world was made good
in the eyes of the attendant

while the bombs beneath
our bulky coats
were only a handbag away

Phobic

where she can't go
is outside then the inside
of this room must do

she travels to its window
cars stop start up
the trains go by

she travels to the white door
A Defence: she opens it only
to close herself in again

she sits beneath the window
she sits beside the radiator
far from the window

the carpet is square a round
ball sound beats
the pavement outside. Perhaps she…?

she closes the open window
Can she maintain this strong
imprisonment, surely she can't?

but the outside, unpredictable
as panic, as her guts churning,
is where multiplication –

never subtraction or complete
removal of machines or people –
occurs – people like ants like

fears, reproduced and reproducing
in a moving mass of many
minute particular ants

upon the concrete yet impossible
patio outside yet inside her head

Small Town Baby

Small Town Baby
I pity you
with your square doughy face
and the life you lead
submerged in pram or push-chair beneath
the very frilled weight of
                                    excessive coverings

Euch! your regal outings
cut no iced cake with me
You are an anachronism in 1993
boy in blue
girl in pink

& then a little older
you trot overdressed
with granny to the shops
a little girl gazing into
her gleaming black patent shoes
having to guard against dirt
on her white socks
the collar is round your neck
lacy enough

There is marriage ahead of you
swaddling of your own infants
& many washes on the whites cycle
of your automatic
Babies bundles of pride
while your life drips
like the tap you leave
for your husband to fix

that boy in blue
that boy in grubby blue
brought on to do
what men should do

Cat's Ear

cat's ear
cat's silence
cat's perfection
looking out
scanning the twilight
through his searching eyes

cat's reflection
and a nearly full moon
above in the sky
where still, birds sing

cat's yawn
a soft afternoon over
visitors gone

Search, pussycat,
amongst the scented wallflowers
the trees in blossom

in the park
I searched this afternoon
for what
was not arid,
dust, forgotten

Untitled

somewhere nowhere
our baby is, is not
perpetual contradiction
always remembered

will always be seen
in our mind's eye
as he was on the ultrascan
superb TV personality

somewhere nowhere
something remains
what I did then
what I do now
what I have become

a stone angel sits
crying in a photo
I cut out from a paper
how, accurately, I chose
grief for a dead child

somewhere nowhere
pointlessness absence
total absence
people have children
we do not have

somewhere nowhere
is here, this land
where children's minds
articulate what
we're not allowed to hear

three sons, three children
this father goes shopping
my world has not got
such swift particulars

we draw in our heads
the social contract, silence
something wrong subtracted
from us looms abstract

a lack child
lessness a death
before there was
a formed enough child

somewhere nowhere
we know our place
our trackless
yet still resisting place

not only do we
insist on why
what happened did
we insist on why

this isolation a mist
a fog we whirl insist
don't you know of us?
we'll tell you

Turn of the Year

Glassy-eyed hopefuls scan
The bleary sky. Another
Year stretches forward, band
Of sullen days on washing lines.

The coal cursed beach throws
Up its Hogmanay of filth;
Fetid sanitary pads, dog shit. They own
This: a marvellous distasteful waste.

Bring down the housewives:
Hoovers suck up lives. Nozzles,
Limp phalluses can't oblige. Wise
Beyond their deaths, the hopefuls

Watch pestilence jam
The hoover spouts. Where are the lacy
Lies now, covering the damned
Clean windows? As machines pump out

Water, clogged with froth,
Detergent broths, horizons
Nowhere here beside the Forth.
All that's recycled is the waste

Of lives. Unemployed stacks,
They'd fill supermarket
Shelves from Heaven to Hell. Go back
Hopefuls from this beach – home.

Homes are the shrines, clothed
And closed against the world.
Framed family members fitted on
The walls will be your community

Of souls. The New Year's
Tongue's a French kiss gone
Sour and sick on too much beer
And nostalgia laden whisky.

Go home, hopefuls or end
It here: the belched up beach,
Its coal seams beneath, unused, can't mend
Misery but only meet it with another

Grumbling New Year.

Shift-Worker

the shifts shunt
us into sidings
of tiredness – gasping
at another irritant,
a barking dog
a revving car
we drag ourselves
through the calendar
of the slow year
towards Xmas,
no bright star

only the fear
of the repossessed house
the kids squalling for
computer games
we can't afford

the street lamp
cups its orange light
as I leave at six
for the early shift
cups its orange light
as I return at 2 a.m.
from the back-shift

like a curled up cat
to me
its permanence
its prettiness

my wife leaves
our bed at 7

I sometimes stroke
nothing on the
confused island
of broken sleep

Martin

Carrying carrier bags of poetry
Morgan Milton Donne
Martin returns to Dunfermline

The night is wet
rain soaks his anorak his face
he can't stop for a drink

two buses away into the night
is home and a shelf of books:
poems, hooks for his anorak

and scarf and hopes
Youths at his stance
suck on dope and shout 'Fuck'

Martin doesn't hear: extra-
galactic warriors breast domed seas
Into his universe comes

the bus to Kirkcaldy
underwater windows, bewildering
signs Then a wait

for the Land-bus to Dunfermline
such a journey to take
to read out loud

sounds like
            Sigmoid foxes at home on rugs
Martin comes home now
with Morgan Milton Donne

'Watch over me,' he says
watering the Poetry Tree
at the foot of his thick-tendrilled bed

before
       Sleep comes, and the clearing
calls where many fruits in plump
agony push out

another of the same. Fruit
begets fruit begets fruit
in Martin's brain

First Visit to Dunfermline

snow
barely noticeable
lands on the neck of a gargoyle
whose home is the Town House wall

even on the hard grey stone
of the gargoyle's thick extended neck
the first few snowflakes melt

it's the same for these snowflakes
landing on the Abbey wall
they melt too, they have possessed
a shorter life than the dead buried here

but the wind, for once, dies down
the Bridges in the distance stand
strangely-shaped skeletons

they wait for flesh to clothe them
it is snow that falls

snow flooring doorways
turning hilly streets into ski-slopes
snow creating a pointy hat on top
of the gargoyle's glowering head

snow settling in necklaces
down the green coppery spire in the distance

snow making sure the Park shrubs
are wrapped up well in white –
their new school uniform

snow zinging in snowballs in playgrounds
snow getting free rides
on the top of the red-and-cream Fife buses

snow, no longer dreaming of a landing,
worrying about a welcome, but
snow
covering all there is to know and see in Dunfermline.

What Went Wrong?

Large tongues of water
Are thrust out
As though to be examined by a doctor.
They lie for a moment
On the dirty, mossy stone
Before they are pulled back
Into their watery home.

Below the surface of the sea, I see
A sign: white letters on red say
ROAD CLOSED
There is no way out through the sea-bed.

So I go to Presto's Supermarket
And buy ten fish-fingers
And return to the sea
And throw them in, one by one, praying
Reconstitute these
Into a Fish God
And the sea does and He appears
And says to me, his love
Come live with me
Come live with me
Come live with me
And be a Human amongst the Cod.

Because I have nothing to lose but nothing
I reply, I WILL
And where there is a will, there is a way
And I find myself in Presto's Supermarket
In the deep freezer amongst the fish,
Marked HUMAN – a very special dish.

Ravenscar

Vertiginous drop down
tree-clad purple heather growing
cliff wooded prehistoric
dream medieval mystery
Victorian challenge yellow
dandelions wind-blown
roses stretching out thorny
branches close to the fall

Rather than descend
to the sea in late Victorian
times it was planned
to terrace these unscaled
heights to plant formal
gardens to encourage promenading

some who reach down
for wisdom some who organise
busy human forms
some who feed the hungry
some who search the unknown
some who investigate muddle

amongst grasses and dog-rose
beside dandelion and cricket
beside whirring fly and thorns
baker and maid at Raven Hall
lay down, stretched minds
no farther than the element of ice
that lay –
with the eerie calmness of the sea
but darker in its reflections –
below them
frozen water
from God's spilled cup

Sarah Oliver, dead, bones,
flesh taking on formlessness,
sex was sweet – rain seeping
into minds not really Church bound

as the black bull got up
onto the brown and white cow
in Springfield's far field
as lambs sucked at full udders
as the horses' shapely forms
filled dreams – a carriage, Sarah,
a carriage is coming up the drive!

Baker, Tom, fat handed Tom,
kitchen Tom, white-apronned Tom,
remembering the thorn entangled
in Sarah's long loosened hair
More loaves than ever, Tom!
As four carriages clatter to a halt.

and what does this do
to us? miscarriages still rattle
in the night surprise the days
disrupt guest-house schedules
lives forming blurt out their mess
and confusion dulls days
but gives us the benefit
of a late breakfast in our B & B
as the landlady must go
to her shaken friend –
I know how that friend feels

creatures meet each other
foetus shaped like fossil
slow snail trails merging
into long horse snouts
snorting in our dreams

the frothless sea resists
passion – the wooded slopes
suck imagination into the tops of trees
that appear green tufts from up here

an abandoned idea
the broad road laid gave
a sense of pioneering, simmering
hopes, laying tarmac on fields
the large Victorian buildings
with a row of shops would sell
and land plots would as well
to men and women off the train

some schemes abort, stopped
by essences beyond transformation
resisting visualising business men

though full of free sherry
those who were to buy
did not take to the forbidding
cliffs to the drop down
to wooded sheer cliff-
sides the gulls in possession
outstretched wings careening
near to hats and crisp maps

below these fields, edging
the cliffs, once thorny dog-roses
are clipped back, once shrubs
and trees are uprooted once
once dreams once plans

to promenade on these terraces
visualised by late Victorian
entrepreneurs – would be to watch
what? – not as in Whitby the sails
of explorers' fleets setting out
for distant lands nor ships
bringing in exotic cargo

here only the waves over boulders
the stunned silence of thick
growth nature not subsumed
rich defiant intractable

there is always some aspect
of the cliff-face in shadow
a dark shadow darkening
tones of trees – oh, I'll be sick

and Emma, Anna, Mariana,
names streaming like gulls
across the sky – halt – it's for
you the entrepreneurs imagine it

in this wind-blown desolation
the empty fripperies of female
life clear-cut as the broad road
statement through fields

abandoned Victorian dream
scheme aborted – grass growing
over station platform steps

Victorian Female Servant

I who am
Come to this great house,
I who am
Lifted to this great house,
Worn down by poverty,
Keen with gratefulness,
I who am –
Thank you, sir, ma'am.

I who am
To share of a very neat room,
Window overlooks
Such a garden and
I who am
With others, watch the others.
I who am –
Thank you, sir, ma'am.

In the steaming kitchen
The boiled birds' beaks hiss
In your pies.
I who am
Serve as best I can, lay
The ballroom bright and grand,
Your glove, sir,
Thank you, sir – no, ma'am.

I who am
Shriek from the roof
'They are bats
These men in frock coats!'
Moving motionless,
Heavy homelessness,
My child – his
Underbellies this.

I who am
Less pretty not neat,
I who am
Hooked, my method
Metal knows
Birth as brief as death.
I who was,
Am, sir!

Out of the Urn

out of the urn
comes the body
head first
tight curls loosening
scarves of blood spiralling away
then a white arm
outstretched towards
migrating birds

out of the urn
comes the body
neck
sloping
to shoulders
then the back

turning half
towards us
on seeing the sun
on seeing the
birds fly free
breasts are seen
full breasts
small mountains

out of the urn
comes the body
nothing pulls it back
down
into that stifling
beneath
now buttocks come
large fast

out of the urn
comes the body
when its feet are
free
they are dancing feet
lithe and neat
and nimble
oh they are
dancing feet!

the body
slips down the
cool glazed patterned
side of the urn
stands
on the ground
feels how warm the grass is

all the birds
are around
flying flying
in the sky
and the biggest
bird is there
just above her
amazed head
big-winged
shadow-ridden
yet not the monster
that it was –
once
it took her in
its beak
and it put her in
a cot
and then
she was buried

now the bird is
out above her
flying in the sky
and its children
are these little birds
that fly away
and she is free

free body
free body
free body
feel the light
blue and shaftlike
is the light
blue and glorious
is this morning
free body
free body
feel the light!

Museums

Museums
are keen on

eyes peering at
white labels
with minute black print on them

and eyes peering at
a truncheon, a patterned plate,
a black case, a brown leather wallet,
an open-barrelled gun, unloaded,
beside it 2 shiny bullets, a book,
another book, another wallet
all in one glass coffin
                with the lid on it.

Sometimes
emotion is at hand –
a tragic love affair
spins in a spiral
out, beyond the glass
and the fine letters
                of grief become our vocabulary

But usually categories of
                era
                make
                material
                theme
                apply.

Never, never
have
all the blue, blue
                objects of the past
swept like a sea
into one museum room.

Return Journey

Take the train back into uncertainty
Ask yourself – Could I? Should I have stayed?
Burn the past into your brain.
Make its buildings bigger, its streets busier,
Its turns of phrase
Returning turns of phrase.

Visit all its pubs.
Remember all its songs.
Burn the past into your brain.
These bright remains are bright because
The fire that burnt you up one day
That glowing, puzzling, strange old flame
Still burns you up today.

I wonder why
You took the train away, that day.
What, in your past, was charred and grey?

Scattering Ashes

I have
your ashes
flung out across your father's grave.
The North Sea pounded below, a deep fished sea.

The birds from the nearby sanctuary
made wheels in the air

and the glassless windows in the churchyard
gave long blue presents of the sea and sky.

Cold day for travelling yet we came. Away
from something dead and thin,

I found a solid poetry in that ruined church
and a conviction of where you returned to

through fire to dust to fire
for your silent nature was garrulous that day
your granite walls flung out sparks skywards –

where hands touched dust, the world was vivid –
specks of fiery ash whirling, merging, painting
all the pictures you didn't paint.

I ignored
my mother's troubled sadness
(the plastic container upset her)

I have
your ashes
warm pride against my cheek as fatherless I sleep
for who would have thought you had it in you

for such a homecoming? Buchan bound:
cliffs standing being eaten by the waves,
froth moving to the greedy plunge of gulls,
destruction and erosion saved by knowing
we return a soul singing in the bird's mouth.

I am Earth

I am Earth

where bulbs are pushed down under my soil,
where they will develop and finally appear,
sharp shoots, pale green in colour,
above my surface.

I am Earth

where roots extend, far below my surface.
These roots grip me, spreading out
their limbs, their fingers through me.
Hard to dig up and pull out, these roots
hold the trees and shrubs and flowers to me.
Through these roots, I feed
the leaves and apples on the tree,
the bright red berries on the shrub,
the pale white petals of Christmas roses.

I am Earth

I receive the dead in their coffins.
Spades have sliced through me
and made a deep space, temporarily, in me.
The words of a prayer hover over me,
the ropes rub against me
as the dead one comes in beside me.
'Dust to dust, ashes to ashes'
A handful of myself settles on the coffin lid.

The years pass. Decay, dissolution occurs
and the dead through me
are re-routed into these,
mauve crocuses streaked with white
opening up on a spring morning
closing as night falls.
These are my flowers.

I am Earth
the powerful strong snug dark place
home of decay and growth.

Liquid Light

There is a liquid light
      that comes from the earth's heart
Even what rots is golden
                then is brown
Handfuls of the black soft stuff
             come from whatever
You know as heaven
        Dark caressing exercising
             the body

There is a liquid light
        glancing on the fir tree's flounces
A liquid light lifting out
        the orange badges of the marigolds
Lines lead to depths
     and shadows
           Earth stays brown
Waiting to be dug
        The light drowns

An autumn day
       beneath the Himalayas of
          white sloped clouds
Rain collects but doesn't fall
         no shipwreck
Autumn is a ship
       sailing on the ground

The colours – red a deep
          pink brown a yellow
Like a china cup you must be careful with
          – its fineness
Russet on a tree
       drawing on a dark red blood

Always orange bright
                    absurd and mottled fallen leaves
The liquid light pours
                    like curves but holds
Steady, for the eternity
                    of now, these gardens
Autumn's cargoes sailing
                    on the soil's dark sea.

The Moon's Leopard

the moon's leopard prowls tonight
feet through vapoury gleaming light
the moon's leopard looks for clues
for where Tom has gone to
Tom   Tom

as though hanging memories on the line
it seems we mourners are coping fine
really we look for God or Death
when there's only the moon's leopard's breath
Tom   Tom

in the forest of the leopard's mind
by the glaciers he left behind
in the fiery clearings made
everywhere – Tom's body was laid
Tom   Tom

the moon's leopard finds glass
in a round white ball on the fabulous grass
the leopard's tongue licks the cool
surface the glass ball becomes a pool
Tom   Tom

here Tom lies here Tom swims
first he's one, then there's many hims
sad delight but magnificent sight
the moon's leopard brings us Tom tonight
Tom   Tom

Country Life

Dead seagull
on the beach.
Dead vole
on the field-path.
Dead rabbit
on the road.
A thrush breaks its neck
against the glass kitchen door.

We don't need to bury
the seagull on the beach,
the vole on the field-path –
they'll decompose
while cars will run over
the rabbit on the road.
But the thrush, the thrush
against our kitchen door?

I don't want to
open
I don't want to
open
our glass kitchen door.

Unpalatable

While a chicken
is eaten for dinner,
a lion is viewed
in the zoo.
Though a lion could
swallow its keeper,
lions in zoos are
subdued.

If a chicken was
but a bit bigger,
recognised as having
a roar,
we'd insist on
a zoo cage to fit her
when she beat on
her battery box door.

It all began with –
THE LIVER –
slippery and
rather red too
and now I've a
problem with chickens
and a sense
of injustice too.

Why don't we
eat lions in Britain?
I know
there are only a few.
But it would be
a gesture to chickens
from lions
who die in our zoos.

The Bullocks

Really thinking about the bullocks –
their massive bulk, their solid flanks
strong as walls and the way they stand
motionless staring out
at intruders into their green world –

Led to a herd of them choosing
to confront me on my way home,
with hooves hammering on the road
and with wide nostrils like slovenly mouths
snorting and breathing in the cloth on my back.

Though weak-kneed,
forcing myself to walk slowly
between the bullocks
and to breathe deeply and regularly
as large veering bodies outflanked me,
I felt pleased

to have met them.
The animal world can still terrify
and head-butt the human.